TO ELLI, ANGELA, OTELLO, AND TIO.
FLOW LIKE A RIVER AND YOU'LL GET THERE SOMEDAY.

Copyright © 2020 by Maciek Albrecht
Book design by Melissa Nelson Greenberg

Library of Congress Cataloging-in-Publication Data available.
ISBN: 978-1-944903-96-1

Printed in China

10 9 8 7 6 5 4 3 2

Cameron Kids is an imprint of Cameron + Company

CAMERON + COMPANY
Petaluma, California
www.cameronbooks.com

THEY CALL ME RIVER

MACIEK ALBRECHT

cameron kids

I begin as rain.

High above the mountaintop
I fall softly from sky to earth.

They call me River.

I am small.

I am carried along.

I play with fish.

Chase dragonflies.

My world is changing all the time.

So am I.

I grow bigger, move faster,

testing my boundaries.

I shimmer and ripple and curve.

I carve the earth.

Twisting, spinning, splashing, roaring.

I am wonderful and wild.

And when I merge with another,

I move smoothly forward.

I glow.

I grow even more powerful and fast.

I spill over the banks.

I am unstoppable.

Until . . .

I am thrown over the edge.

Suspended for a moment.

Then I am falling,

falling into silence.

I crash and shatter,

resurface in the shadow of an old tree.

Lost.

I move in circles.

Could I have been a lake or a pond?

What if I had floated underground?

Finding my flow again,

I am back in the mainstream.

Millions of lights shine

and I shine.

I reflect the world.

I ease into wide-open,

lonesome landscapes.

The moon keeps me company.

I treasure every drop,

every ripple,

every breath.

I fulfill wishes.

I carry big ships like paper boats.

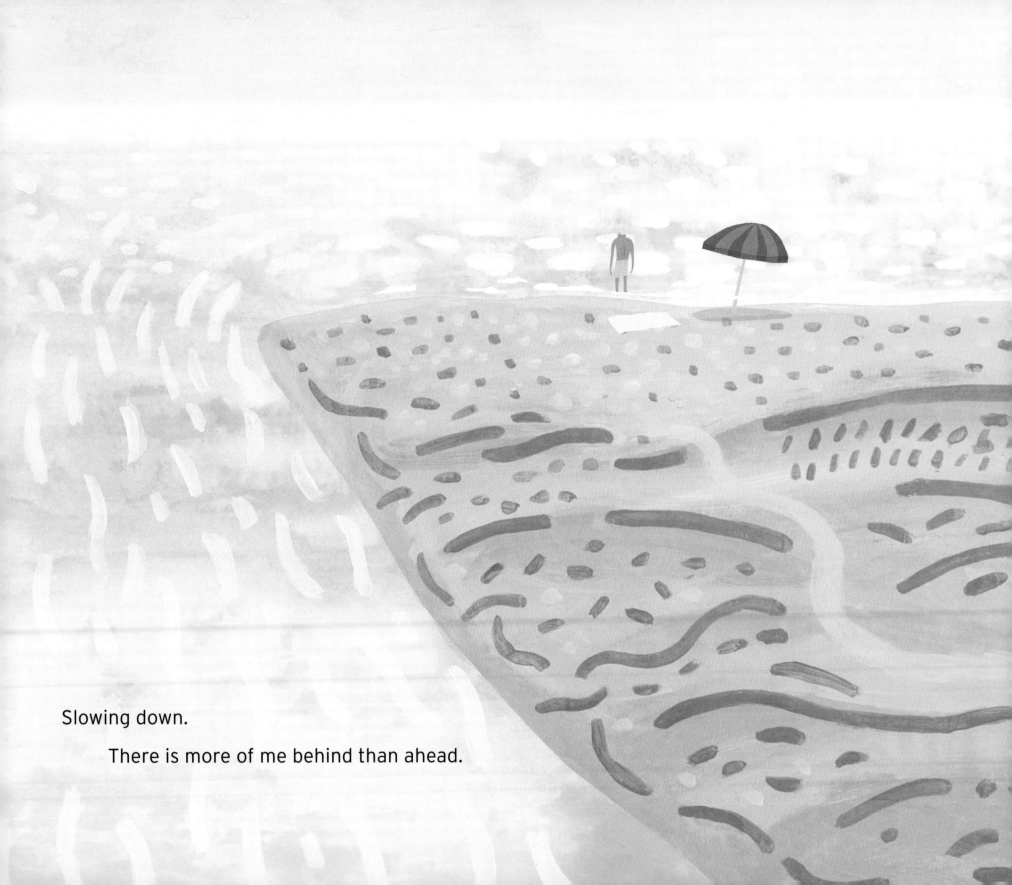

Slowing down.

There is more of me behind than ahead.

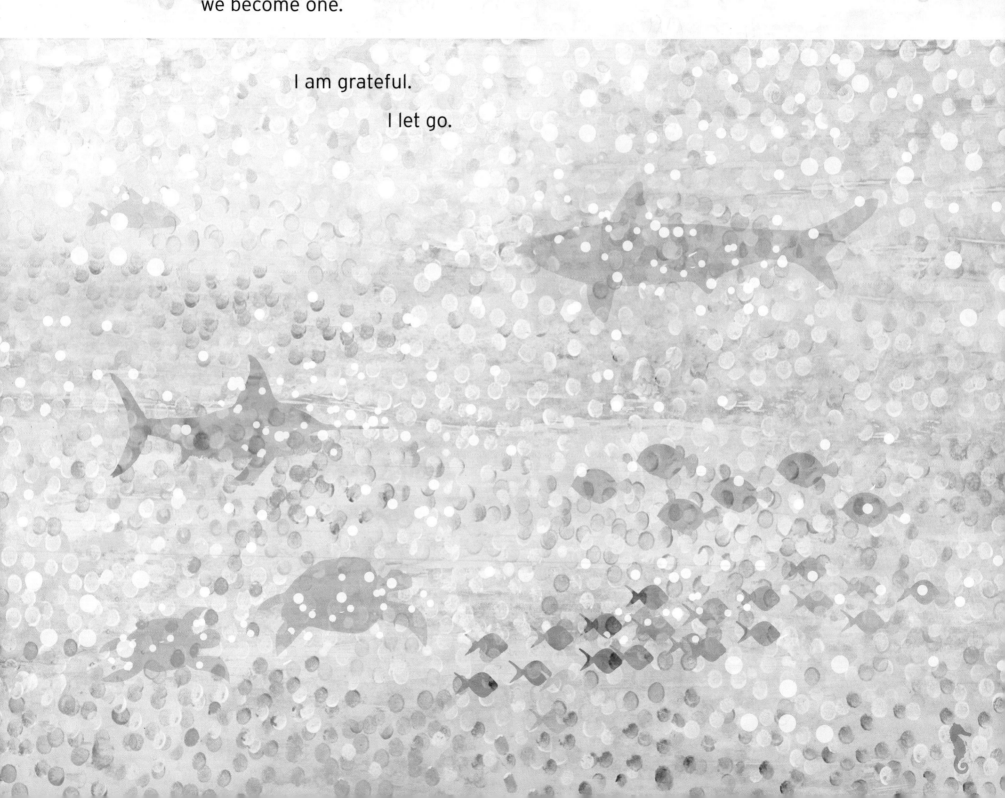

When I meet the great ocean,

we become one.

I am grateful.

I let go.

And then, drop by drop,

I return to the sky.

And I begin again . . .